9780838107133

by Hyman and Alice Chanover

with Illustrations by Leonard Kessler

UNITED SYNAGOGUE COMMISSION
ON JEWISH EDUCATION

COPYRIGHT 1956 BY THE UNITED SYNAGOGUE OF AMERICA
Printed in the United States of America.

PESAḤ IS COMING!

Everybody was busy.

Mommy and Daddy were busy. Grandma and Grandpa were busy. Mimmy and Joel were busy. Even Baby Dan was busy. It was the evening before Pesaḥ, and everybody was preparing for the holiday.

Daddy and Grandpa were in the basement getting ready to bring up the Pesaḥ dishes. Mimmy and Joel and Baby Dan were there, too, helping.

Up the stairs came Daddy and Grandpa carrying a heavy carton filled with pots and pans and dishes, and up the stairs came Mimmy, Joel, and Baby Dan after them with little boxes in their hands. Down and up, down and up they went until all the Pesaḥ things were brought upstairs.

Daddy's hair was all messed up, and he was huffing and puffing. "That was hard work," he said, pushing his hair back from his forehead.

"Yes it was," Joel agreed, as he wiped his face. "But it was fun."

"May we help you open the boxes and cartons now, Daddy?" Mimmy asked. "Of course you may, dear," answered Daddy, but you will be careful, won't you?"

Mimmy and Joel dashed over to Daddy's side. Baby Dan came over to help, too. He looked so cute with his tiny curl dangling down over his forehead. His little blue eyes watched the scissors go "snip, snip," cutting the string on the cartons.

"Snip, snip" they went again and again until all the cartons and boxes were open.

"Ooh, here's our Seder plate, right on top of this carton!" exclaimed Mimmy, as she took the wrappings off a big, beautiful plate. "And look what I found!" cried Joel, pulling out a whole handful of forks and spoons.

Baby Dan was too small to help unpack things, but he was sharing in the work. He was running back and forth, back and forth, from the cartons to the corner of the room, making a huge pile out of the large pieces of wrapping paper.

Suddenly there was a wee little sound from somewhere in the room: *Meow!* Yes, there it was again, only louder this time: *MEOW!*

MEOW MEOW MEOW MEOW

It was Pussy, the brown and white kitten the children had received for Ḥanukah. Everyone started searching for Pussy. They knew she was in the room somewhere, but where? Under the chairs? No. Under the table? No, not there. Behind the door? Pussy was not there, either.

Where could she be?

Just then, a soft, furry little face, with green eyes and long whiskers peeked out at everybody from under the pile of wrapping paper in the corner. Daddy was the first to see Pussy's sleepy little head.

"There's Pussy!" he exclaimed, pointing to the corner, and he began to laugh merrily. Grandpa started to chuckle, too. "Why, Baby Dan," he said, "you must have put all the papers on top of

Pussy while she was sleeping!" Joel and Mimmy thought that was very funny. They couldn't stop giggling. Soon everybody was laughing, even Baby Dan.

Pussy shook the papers off her back. She yawned, stretched her little paws, and came over to Mimmy. Then she rubbed her warm, velvety body against Mimmy's leg.

Mimmy bent down to pat her. Suddenly she turned to everybody and said: "I just thought of something. How about getting some new Pesaḥ dishes for our kitten? I'll go and ask Mommy right now!"

Into the kitchen she skipped, her shiny black hair bobbing up and down.

In the kitchen, Mommy and Grandma were very busy washing and wiping the dishes that had been brought up from the basement. Mommy was washing and Grandma was wiping. One . . . two . . . three . . . stacks of dishes were already shiny and clean. They were waiting to be put away in the cabinet which the family had set aside especially for Pesaḥ.

"Mommy," said Mimmy as she entered the room, "I would like to get some Pesaḥ dishes for Pussy, too."

"All right, dear, if you want to," Mommy answered. "While I put Baby Dan to bed, ask Grandpa if he would like to take you and Joel to the store to buy two brand new saucers for Pussy."

"Goody, goody!" Mimmy cried out. And she bounded out of the kitchen to tell Grandpa what Mommy had said. Grandpa smiled. Of course he would be glad to take them!

Grandpa and Mimmy and Joel put on their coats and off to the store the three of them went.

Mr. Levy, the storekeeper, was a round, pudgy man with a big, bushy moustache. "Hello, everybody," he greeted them. "What brings you here this evening?"

"Grandpa brought us so we could buy our kitten some new saucers for Pesaḥ," Mimmy said. "Do you have any yellow ones?"

"I certainly do!" said Mr. Levy, smiling. "And I also have blue ones."

"Let's take one of each," Joel suggested. Mimmy thought that was a good idea. So Grandpa paid for the dishes, and home they went. It was already time for Mimmy and Joel to go to bed.

The next morning, the children could hardly wait until breakfast was over. "How soon may we help you make the Ḥaroset for the Seder?" they asked Mommy. "As soon as you finish eating, and all the Ḥametz dishes are put away," she replied.

"I'll be through in a minute," Joel said, and gulped down the last mouthful of milk. "So will I, called Mimmy as she popped the last piece of cookie into her mouth.

When the table was cleared, they waited for Mommy to tell them how to make Ḥaroset. "The first thing you need is an apple," she said. Mimmy darted over to the refrigerator and took out a round, juicy one. Mommy then cut it into small thin slices.

"What do we need now?" Joel asked eagerly.

"Some walnuts," Mommy told him and handed Joel a nutcracker and a large bag filled with nuts. He began to open one nut after another.

"Will this be enough for Ḥaroset?" he asked a few minutes later. He had already opened ten large nuts.

"Oh yes. More than enough. You may even eat one or two."

Joel was hoping Mommy would say just that. He gave Mimmy one, and, quicker than a squirrel, chewed up the other.

Mommy then took the nuts and the apple slices and put them in a food chopper. "You and Mimmy now may take turns chopping the apple slices and the nuts into very small pieces," she said.

"It's my turn first," Mimmy shouted. "Chop, chop," went the chopper, crushing everything into small pieces.

"You've had the foodchopper long enough," Joel insisted after a while. "Now it's my turn." And he took the handle.

"Chop, chop, scrish scrush," the chopper went again.

Baby Dan climbed up on a chair to watch. His bright blue eyes followed the chopper as it went up and down, up and down.

When the apples and nuts were crushed fine, Mommy took a bottle of delicious purple wine out of the refrigerator. The wine gurgled noisily as it was poured into the foodchopper. Then Mommy sprinkled in some cinnamon.

Again the children chopped. First Mimmy, then Joel. Soon the Ḥaroset was ready.

"Please let us taste it," the children begged. Mommy gave each of them a taste. Mmm. It was delicious!

"Now, Mimmy, please put the Ḥaroset into the refrigerator," said Mommy. "There's lots of work still to be done."

All morning and all afternoon Mommy and Grandma were busy preparing for the Seder. They swept and they dusted. They cooked and they baked.

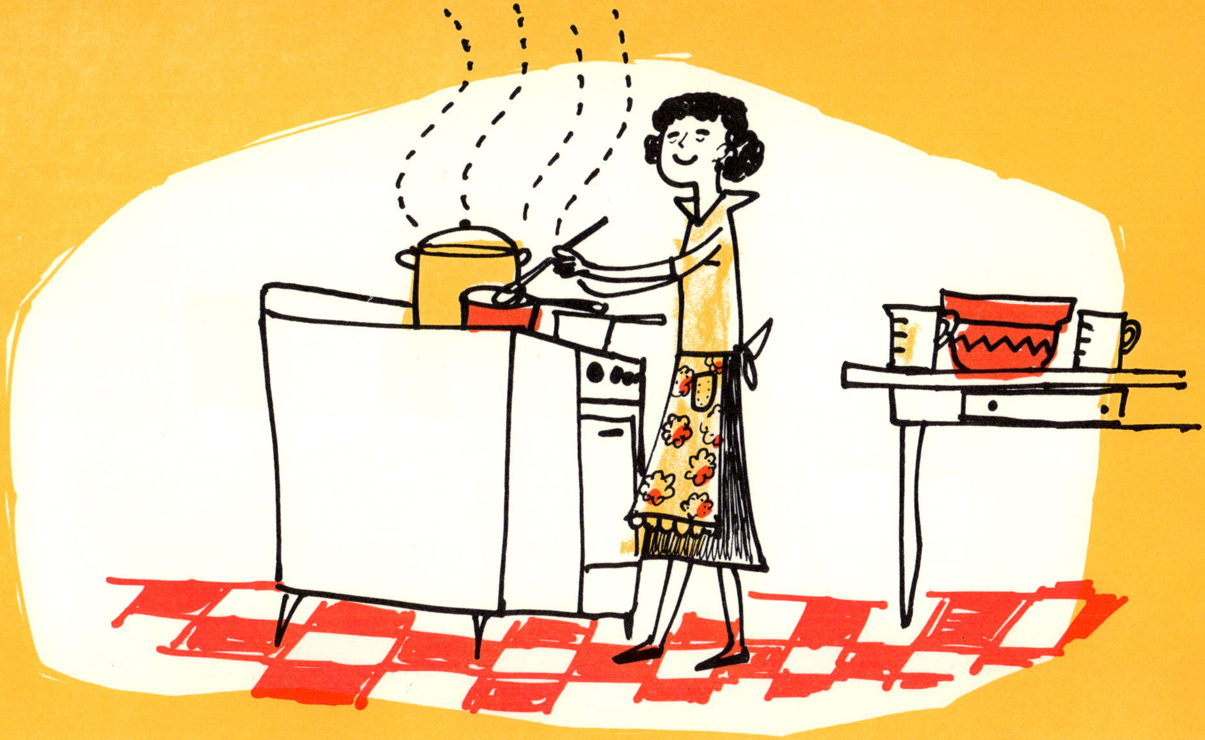

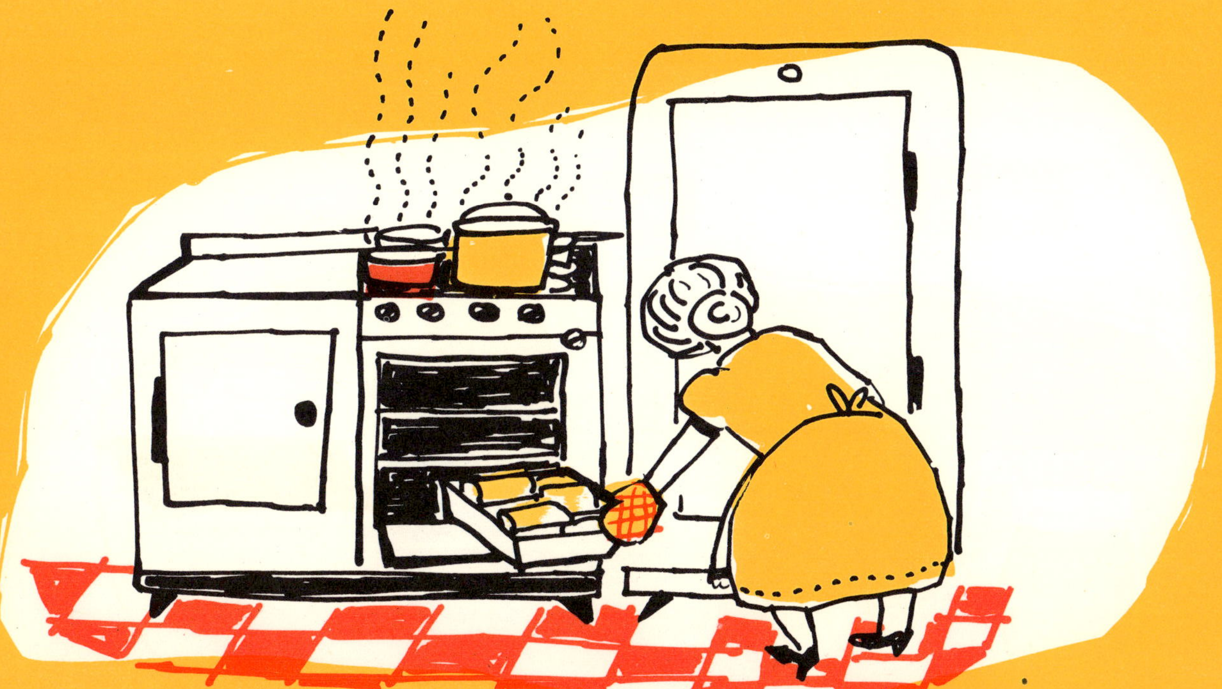

By the time they were finished the house was spick-and-span, and there were many good foods all ready for the Seder—a huge pot of golden chicken soup, and fat, round matzah balls, and rosy red apple sauce, and a large, spicy nut cake.

In the cabinet was a fresh box of matzot waiting to be opened. In the refrigerator were a roasted egg, a roasted meat bone, parsley, and horseradish for the Seder plate. And a bottle of Pesaḥ wine was getting deliciously cold!

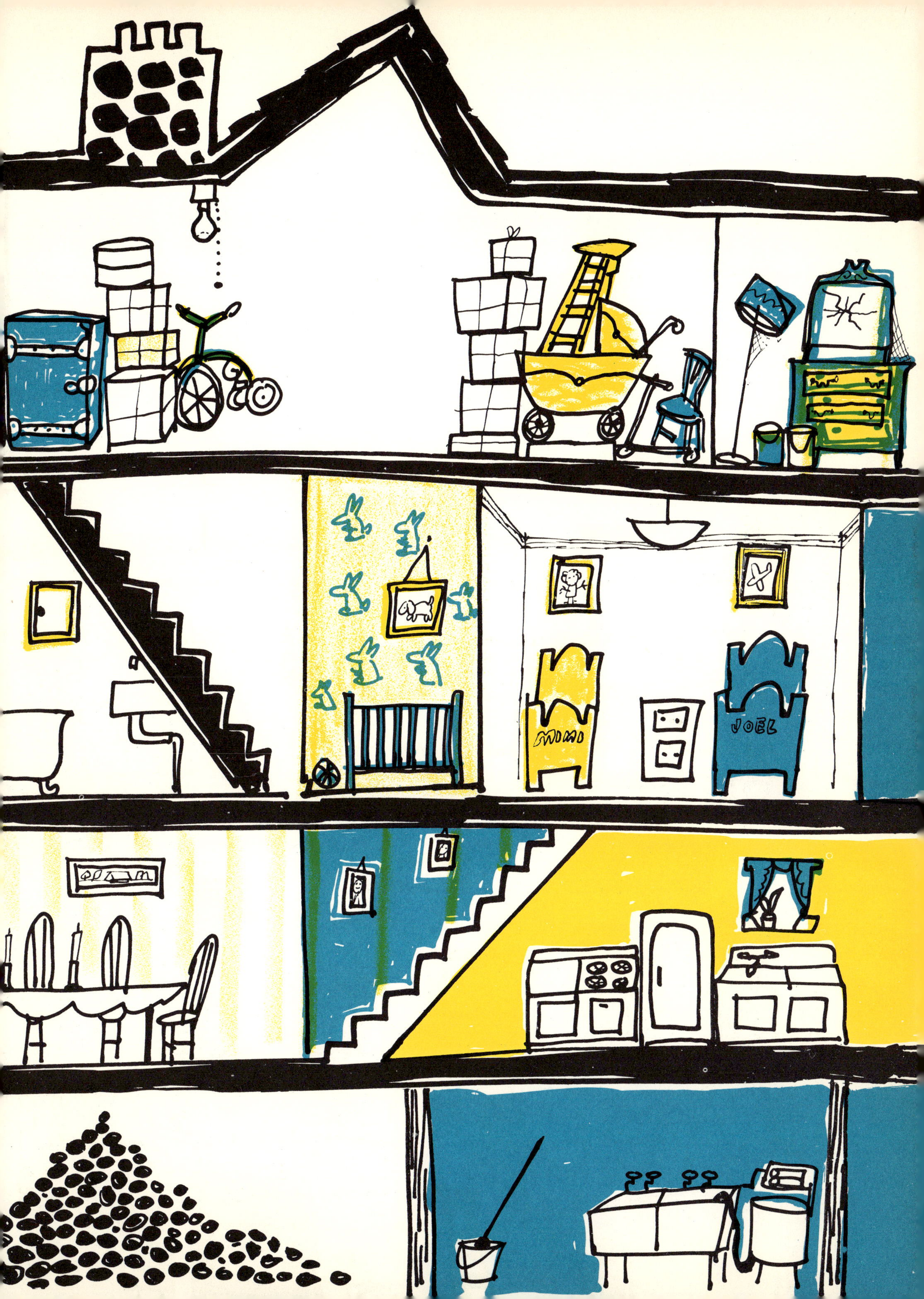
MIMI
JOEL

"Come, children," Mommy called. "Before we set the Seder table, let's all go upstairs and get dressed in our new holiday clothes."

"Yippee!" the children shouted and dashed up the stairs to their rooms.

Mimmy was so excited about her new pink dress that she put it on backwards. Mommy had to help her turn it around.

Joel felt very grown-up putting on his new bow-tie. It was just like Daddy's. And his new shoes squeaked noisily as he walked. Squeak, squeak, squeak, squeak.

There were Pesaḥ clothes for Baby Dan, too: a blue and white suit with a picture of a cute little puppy dog right on the pocket of the shirt.

And there was also something new for Pussy. Can you guess what it was?

A bright yellow ribbon which Mommy tied around her neck.

While the children were brushing and combing their hair, Mimmy sang a lovely song. This is how it went:

Slowly, with vigor

Joy-ous day, Hap-py day, Ḥag Ha-Pe-saḥ is com-ing.
At the Se-der we will dine On the Matz-ot and the wine.
Let's not wait, It's get-ting late, Time to set the Se-der plate.

Yes, it *was* getting late. The sun was beginning to set. Soon it would be time for the Seder—the happy, wonderful Seder.

Glossary

Ḥametz   The term is used to indicate food prepared with leaven, therefore, not permissible for Passover.

Ḥaroset   A pasty compound of apples, nuts, cinnamon, and wine, symbolic of the mortar made by the enslaved Israelites in Egypt.

Seder   The ceremonial meal conducted in traditional Jewish homes on the first two evenings of the Passover holiday.

HAMETZ

HAROSET